OBEYING DIVINE INSTRUCTIONS

"If they obey and serve him, they shall spend their days in prosperity, and their years in pleasures."

Job 36:11

by

Franklin N. Abazie

Obeying Divine Instructions
COPYRIGHT 2017 BY Franklin N Abazie
ISBN: 978-1-945133-36-7

All right reserved. This book or any portion thereof may not be reproduced or used in any manner whatsoever without the express written permission of the publisher, except for the use of brief quotations in a book review. All Bible quotes are from King James Version and others as noted.

Published by: F N ABAZIE PUBLISHING HOUSE- aka, Empowerment Bookstore.

That I may publish with the voice of thanksgiving and tell of all thy wondrous works.
Psalms 26:7

To order additional copies, wholesales
or booking:
Call the Church office (973-372-7518),
or Empowerment Bookstore Hotline (973-393-8518)

Worship address:
343 Sanford Avenue Newark New Jersey 07106
Administrative Head Office address:
33 Schley Street Newark New Jersey 07112
Email:pastorfranknto@yahoo.com
Website www.fnabaziehealingministries.org
Publishing House: www.fnabaziepublishinghouse.org

This book is a production of F N Abazie Publishing House.
A publication Arms of Miracle of God Ministries 2017.
First Edition

CONTENTS

THE MANDATE OF THE COMMISSION iv
ARMS OF THE COMMISSION v
INTRODUCTION vi
CHAPTER 1
1 The Reward of Obedience 1
CHAPTER 2
2 The Mystery of Faithfulness 14
CHAPTER 3
3 Prayer of Salvation 58
CHAPTER 4
4 About The Author 72

THE MANDATE OF THE COMMISSION

"The moment is due to impact your world through the revival of the healing & miracle ministry of Jesus Christ of Nazareth."

"I am sending you to restore health unto thee and I will heal thee of thy wounds, said the Lord of Host."

ARMS OF THE COMMISSION

1) F N Abazie Ministries-Miracle of God Ministries (Miracle Chapel Intl)

2) F N Abazie TV Ministries: Global Television Ministry Outreach

3) F N Abazie Radio Ministries: Radio Broadcasting Outreach

4) F N Abazie Publishing House: Book Publication

5) F N Abazie Bible School: also called Word of Healing Bible School (W.O.H.B.S)

6) F N Abazie Evangelistic Ass: Miracle of God Ministries: Global Crusade

7) Empowerment Bookstore: Book distribution

8) F N Abazie Helping Hands: Meeting the help of the needy world wide

9) F N Abazie Disaster Recovery Mission: Global Disaster Recovery

10) F N Abazie Prison Ministry: Prison Ministry for all convicts "Second chance"

Some of our ministry arms are waiting the appointed time to commence.

FAVOR CONFESSION

Father thank you for making me righteous and accepted through the blood of Jesus Christ. Because of that, I am blessed and highly favored by God. I am the subject of your affection. Your favor surrounds me as a shield, and the first thing that people see around me is your favored shield. Thank you that I have favor with you and man today. All day long people go out of their way to bless me and help me. I have favor with everyone that I deal with today. Doors that were once closed are now opened for me. I receive preferential treatment, and I have special privileges, I am Gods favored child.

No good thing will he withhold from me. Because of Gods favor my enemies cannot triumph over my life. I have supernatural increase and promotion. I declare restoration to everything that the devil has stolen from my life. I have honor in the midst of my adversaries and an increase in assets, especially in real estate and expansion of territories.

Because I am highly favored by God, I experience great victories, supernatural turnarounds, and miraculous breakthrough in the midst of great impossibilities. I receive recognition, prominence, and honor. Petitions are granted to me even by ungodly authorities. Policies, rules, regulations, and laws are changed and reverse on my behalf.

I win battles that I don't even have to fight, because God fights them for me. This is the day, the set time and the designated moment for me to experience the free favor of God, that profusely and lavishly abound on my behalf in Jesus name. Amen.

INTRODUCTION

"My sheep hear my voice, and I know them, and they follow me:"
John 10:27

The mere fact that you are reading this *book is an indication that you genuinely want to obey God's divine instructions concerning your life.* For the most part, this publication is a book of *inspiration and motivation*. The *context of this text is to inspire you to obey the voice of God* with everything inside of you. Unless you *obey God in life*, you will never succeed in the midst of challenges. One great man of God said and I quote, *"the instructions you chose to obey will determine the future you will create."* In my own opinion divine instruction is the gateway into riches and glory. *"Thus saith the Lord, thy Redeemer, the Holy One of Israel; I am the Lord thy God which teacheth thee to profit, which leadeth thee by the way that thou shouldest go."* **Isaiah 48:17**

For unless we *obey His commandment and instructions,* we shall forever struggle and in want of all things in life. For the most part, God has been trying to instruct and direct most of us. *"I will instruct thee and teach thee in the way which thou shalt go: I will guide thee with mine eye."* **Psalms 32:8**

But we are too busy searching for how to fulfill our own heart desires. Every now and then *God will give us a dream*. It is sad to say, how many of us, *obey the divine instruction* we get from God. *"For God speaketh once, yea twice, yet man perceiveth it not. In a dream, in a vision of the night, when deep sleep falleth upon men, in slumberings upon the bed; Then he openeth the ears of men, and sealeth their instruction."* **Job 33:14-16**

Whenever God leads, He *directs and instructs*. *"And they thirsted not when he led them through the deserts: he caused the waters to flow out of the rock for them: he clave the rock also, and the waters gushed out."* **(Isaiah 48:21)** *"If it is not good, then it is not God."* For every time God leads, *He corrects, directs and instructs in righteousness,* what we ought to do, and how we ought to do it. Every time *God leads*, regardless of the prevailing trials and obstacles, we always succeed at the end. It is written, *"Let your conversation be without covetousness; and be content with such things as ye have: for he hath said, I will never leave thee, nor forsake thee."* **Hebrew 13:5**

Cut to the chase, unless *you obey divine instructions*, your life will *be full of struggles, trial, and tribulation.* In this publication you will appreciate *the mystery of obeying divine instructions in life.* One man said, *"You walk by common sense, you run by principles, but you fly by instructions."* If you must emerge high flyers in life, then you must learn to obey divine instruction.

"For the Lord's portion is his people; Jacob is the lot of his inheritance. He found him in a desert land, and in the waste howling wilderness; he led him about, he instructed him, he kept him as the apple of his eye. As an eagle stirreth up her nest, fluttereth over her young, spreadeth abroad her wings, taketh them, beareth them on her wings: So the Lord alone did lead him, and there was no strange god with him. He made him ride on the high places of the earth, that he might eat the increase of the fields; and he made him to suck honey out of the rock, and oil out of the flinty rock; Butter of kine, and milk of sheep, with fat of lambs, and rams of the breed of Bashan, and goats, with the fat of kidneys of wheat; and thou didst drink the pure blood of the grape." **Deut 32:9-14**

I have tried, as revealed by the Holy Ghost, to unfold some *revelations and instructions* as revealed by God. I guarantee you! Your life will never remain the same as you read this book. God will meet you at your point of need. Let me pray, *Precious Holy Spirit, grant oh Lord this precious one, permission to enjoy your mysteries as you speak to us all through the pages of this small book. In Jesus Mighty Name.* Amen.

HIS DESTINY WAS THE **CROSS**....

HIS PURPOSE WAS **LOVE**.....

HIS REASON WAS **YOU**....

" If they obey and serve him, they shall spend their days in prosperity, and their years in pleasures."

Job 36:11

"If ye be willing and obedient, ye shall eat the good of the land:"

Isaiah 1:19

HOW DO I OBEY DIVINE INSTRUCTION

----*Faith in God*

Divine instruction is a function of our faith in God. Others *may hear from God and ignore it*. But every time you hear from God and obey His instructions by taking action, you secure His divine blessings. It is written, *"For whatsoever is born of God overcometh the world: and this is the victory that overcometh the world, even our faith."* **1 John 5:4**

----*We must be expectant*

We must always expect God to do the impossible for us in life. It is written, *"Who seeing Peter and John about to go into the temple asked an alms. And Peter, fastening his eyes upon him with John, said, Look on us. And he gave heed unto them, expecting to receive something of them. Then Peter said, Silver and gold have I none; but such as I have give I thee: In the name of Jesus Christ of Nazareth rise up and walk."* **Acts 3:3-6**

Expectation is the secured foundation for the manifestation of the Power of God. If we must experience anything in life we must expect it from God. Anybody can chose to obey, but unless you expect to hear from God, the miracle will not be stirred up.

----*We must be willing*

No one can lie or hide from God. Often some folks pretend to obey their own voice rather *than seek for divine direction*. It is easy to obey what we want to do. But unless we obey God from a willing spirit we will not be able to receive the supernatural miracles in stock for us in life. It is written, *"If ye be willing and obedient, ye shall eat the good of the land:"* **Isaiah 1:19**

Every time we do anything willingly in life, it comes with a reward from God. Apostle Paul said, *"For if I do this thing willingly, I have a reward: but if against my will, a dispensation of the gospel is committed unto me."* (1 Cor 9:17)

Often we suffer difficulties in life, not because we are not willing, but because we are ignorant of the truth. It is written, *"My people are destroyed for lack of knowledge: because thou hast rejected knowledge, I will also reject thee, that thou shalt be no priest to me: seeing thou hast forgotten the law of thy God, I will also forget thy children."* **Hosea 4:6**

It takes the revelation of the word of God, to gain understanding, correction, and instruction.

We are also told...

"Therefore my people are gone into captivity, because they have no knowledge: and their honourable men are famished, and their multitude dried up with thirst." **Isaiah 5:13**

CHAPTER 1
THE REWARD OF OBEDIENCE

"If ye be willing and obedient, ye shall eat the good of the land:"
Isiah 1:19

In my own opinion, *to obey God is a choice we make in life.* Often *most of us hear from God but disobey heavely instructions.* If anyone must go higher and make an *impact in life, we must repent,* and obey the voice of God. *"If my people, which are called by my name, shall humble themselves, and pray, and seek my face, and turn from their wicked ways; then will I hear from heaven, and will forgive their sin, and will heal their land."* **2 Chr 7:14**

If I am permitted to put it this way, *the blessings of God are hidden in obedience.* For unless *we obey the voice of God in life,* we will never emerge as high-flyers in life. Unless *we obey God we* will never make an impact in our generation. One man said and I quote, *"the instructions you chose to obey will determine the future that you will create."*

DIVINE INSTRUCTION IS THE GATEWAY TO GREATNESS

Jesus Christ made it crystal clear, when He said, *"follow me and I will make you."* *"And he saith unto them, Follow me, and I will make you fishers of men."* **Matthew 4:19**

You cannot go wrong following the *leading of Jesus.* You cannot be struggling in life, if *you are following the instruction of God.* Every time God leads, He clears the obstacles before anyone. *"Thus saith the Lord, thy Redeemer, the Holy One of Israel; I am the Lord thy God which teacheth thee to profit, which leadeth thee by the way that thou shouldest go."* **Isaiah 48:17**

We were told....

"And they thirsted not when he led them through the deserts: he caused the waters to flow out of the rock for them: he clave the rock also, and the waters gushed out." **Isaiah 48:21**

OBEDIENCE IS BETTER THAN SACRIFICE

It is written, *"And Samuel said, Hath the Lord as great delight in burnt offerings and sacrifices, as in obeying the voice of the Lord? Behold, to obey is better than sacrifice, and to hearken than the fat of rams."* **1 Samuel 15:22**

I like to admonish *you to obey the voice of God*. May I persuade *you to obey divine instruction concerning your life.* Quite often we are very stubborn *to obey* what *God is saying* to us. *"For rebellion is as the sin of witchcraft, and stubbornness is as iniquity and idolatry. Because thou hast rejected the word of the Lord, he hath also rejected thee from being king."* **1 Samuel 15:23**

Remember....

Every time *you disobey the voice of God,* you give away your blessing and kingship. Remember *we are called to rule and to reign* on earth. God said, *"By me king's reign, and princes decree justice."* **Proverb 8:15**

Every time we reject the word of God, we close up our opportunity to break through in life. It is written, *"... Because thou hast rejected the word of the Lord, he hath also rejected thee from being king."* **1 Samuel 15:23**

God has made us Kings *"And hast made us unto our God kings and priests: and we shall reign on the earth."* **(Rev 5:10)** *Abraham became great because he obeyed the voice of God.* God only rewards our obedience in life. If you must become great in life, then you must submit to *obey divine instruction*.

We were told....

"Ye have seen what I did unto the Egyptians, and how I bare you on eagles' wings, and brought you unto myself. Now therefore, if ye will obey my voice indeed, and keep my covenant, then ye shall be a peculiar treasure unto me above all people: for all the earth is mine:" **(Exodus 19:4-5)** As complicated as it may sound, righteousness is the fruit of obedience. Have you not heard? *"Follow peace with all men, and holiness, without which no man shall see the Lord:"* **Hebrew 12:14**

Often so many of us hear the word daily, yet we do not obey the voice of God. Whatever blessing, we will ever desire in life is hidden in our ability to obey, and yield to divine instruction.

A typical example is the Sermon on the Mount.

"Blessed are the poor in spirit: for theirs is the kingdom of heaven.

Blessed are they that mourn: for they shall be comforted.

Blessed are the meek: for they shall inherit the earth.

Blessed are they which do hunger and thirst after righteousness: for they shall be filled.

Blessed are the merciful: for they shall obtain mercy.

Blessed are the pure in heart: for they shall see God.

Blessed are the peacemakers: for they shall be called the children of God.

Blessed are they which are persecuted for righteousness' sake: for theirs is the kingdom of heaven.

Blessed are ye, when men shall revile you, and persecute you, and shall say all manner of evil against you falsely, for my sake.

Rejoice, and be exceeding glad: for great is your reward in heaven: for so persecuted they the prophets which were before you." **Matthew 5:3-12**

In the above passages, we are told what to do, and the reward that follows. *"Only if we obey."* In my opinion *obedience is a mystery of life.* For no *man will obey God and still remain the same.* Jesus said, *"He that hath my commandments, and keepeth them, he it is that loveth me: and he that loveth me shall be loved of my Father, and I will love him, and will manifest myself to him."* **John 14:21**

Remember....

"By this we know that we love the children of God, when we love God, and keep his commandments. For this is the love of God, that we keep his commandments: and his commandments are not grievous." **1 John 5:2-3**

It is a shame to answer a Christian, yet our life does not reflect the same. The dignity of our Christianity must become evidence of our walk with Christ. For no man can walk with God and remain the same. God *rewards us according to our level of obedience to His Holy Scripture.* Every Christian with a character problem has not genuinely repented. Every ministry over-seer with a scandal hanging all over him/her, have not genuinely repented. Every time the light of God genuinely enters any man/woman it reflects like a mirror. The light of God and darkness cannot co-exist together in any life.

Every time the light of God, genuinely enters anyone heart, darkness (evil & immoralities) must be evicted out of that life.

Have you not read?

"Be not overcome of evil, but overcome evil with good." **Romans 12:21**

Have you not read?

"The evil bow before the good; and the wicked at the gates of the righteous." **Proverb 14:19**

We are told from John chapter one verse one. *"In the beginning was the Word, and the Word was with God, and the Word was God. The same was in the beginning with God. All things were made by him; and without him was not anything made that was made. In him was life; and the life was the light of men. And the light shineth in darkness; and the darkness comprehended it not."*

Although God gave us *the power of choice* but we must *consciously become Christians by the conviction of the Holy*

Spirit. We live in an evil generation where the propaganda for sin and immoralities have captured every media network from the television, to the newspapers, radio, to magazine.e.t.c. But for those of us that are still holding on to the integrity of our Christianity, God promises to vindicate us from the trials and tribulation of life.

In my opinion it takes a heart and love for God to become *a man or woman of God. It takes a heart of obedience to maintain the dignity of our Christianity.* Realize with me, that you cannot fool God. *"The fool hath said in his heart, There is no God. They are corrupt, they have done abominable works, there is none that doeth good. The Lord looked down from heaven upon the children of men, to see if there were any that did understand, and seek God. They are all gone aside, they are all together become filthy: there is none that doeth good, no, not one."* **Psalms 14:1-3**

"Have all the workers of iniquity no knowledge? Who eat up my people as they eat bread, and call not upon the Lord. **(Psalms 14:4)** Anyone who is not living right for God, it is only a question of time, and they shall be exposed by the Holy Spirit.

THE REWARD OF OBEDIENCE

~LONG LIFE

If we live according to *the will of God and obey His laws*, automatically our days will be lengthened. In the same vein, if we disobey God, and live a reckless life, eventually our days will be shortened. *And ye shall serve the Lord your God, and he shall bless thy bread, and thy water; and I will take sickness away from the midst of thee. There shall nothing cast their young, nor be barren, in thy land: the number of thy days I will fulfill.* **Exodus 23:25-26**

We were promised....

"With long life will I satisfy him, and shew him my salvation." **Pslams 91:16**

~PROTECTION

It is written, *"For he shall give his angels charge over thee, to keep thee in all thy ways."* **(Psalms 91:11)** God protects us only when we are under the covenant. It is written, *And who is he that will harm you, if ye be followers of that which is good? Every time we obey the commandment, we secure His protection over our lives and properties.*

Remember....

"Whoso keepeth the commandment shall feel no evil thing: and a wise man's heart discerneth both time and judgment." **Eccl 8:5**

~GOOD HEALTH

Often most people are sick, not because they do not eat healthy, or because of some strange disease, but because they are under tension. Every time you live in stress, you live in sickness. Every time you live in sin you live in sickness. In my own opinion, it takes a merry heart to remain healthy. We are told, *"A merry heart doeth good like a medicine: but a broken spirit drieth the bones."* **Proverb 17:22**

It is written, *"The spirit of a man will sustain his infirmity; but a wounded spirit who can bear?"* **Proverb 18:14**

It is the joy of the Lord that gives us strength to endue all prevailing temptation in life. Obedience to the word of God is the foundation to good health.

~CONFIDENCE

Every time you develop the habit to *obey God, you develop self confidence.* It is written, *"If they obey and serve him, they shall spend their days in prosperity, and their years in pleasures."* **Job 36:11**

~PROMOTION

Often some of us thinks that breakthrough and promotion comes by our personal abilities. Unless you obey God you will never experience the promotion of that comes from the Lord. It is written, *"For promotion cometh neither from the east, nor from the west, nor from the south."* **Psalms 75:6**

~UNLIMITED INSIGHT

God grants us unlimited insight every time we live in obedience. It is my prayer that you develop *the lifestyle of obedience to the things of God. Every time you operate in obedience you* gain insight and deep knowledge of the things of the spirit.

~WISDOM

Anyone *obeying divine leading of the Holy Spirit operates in divine wisdom.* This is the *wisdom from above* that gives us understanding in all things. It is written, *"But the wisdom that is from above is first pure, then peaceable, gentle, and easy to be intreated, full of mercy and good fruits, without partiality, and without hypocrisy."* **James 3:17**

It was *divine wisdom* that helped David to prevail against the assaults of King Saul. We were told of how David possessed the wisdom of an angel. Recall, *"To fetch about this form of speech hath thy servant Joab done this thing: and my lord is wise, according to the wisdom of an angel of God, to know all things that are in the earth."* **2 Samuel 14:20**

"And Saul was afraid of David, because the Lord was with him, and was departed from Saul. Therefore Saul removed him from him, and made him his captain over a thousand; and he went out and came in before the people. And David behaved himself wisely in all his ways; and the Lord was with him. Wherefore when Saul saw that he behaved himself very wisely, he was afraid of him." **1 Samuel 18:12-15**

If I am permitted to say it this way. Every commandment we *obey* puts us in command of all things. *"If you must become a commander then you must obey the instructions of the Lord."* Everyone in need of *divine wisdom* must *first repent for God to restore his/her life.* Anyone *seeking divine wisdom must obey divine instructions.*

It is written....

"If any of you lack wisdom, let him ask of God, that giveth to all men liberally, and upbraideth not; and it shall be given him. But let him ask in faith, nothing wavering. For he that wavereth is like a wave of the sea driven with the wind and tossed." **(James 1:5-6)** God will gives us wisdom only when we ask Him in faith, and in obedience of His word.

CHAPTER 2

THE MYSTERY OF FAITHFULNESS

*"Faithful is he that calleth you,
who also will do it."*
1 Theo 5:24

Faithfulness is a mystery of obedience. For no man can become faithful in life, without diligent obedience, faith, and totally obeying divine instructions. Obedience to the instruction of God is a function of faithfulness. Talking about Abraham, when God instructed him, he faithfully obeyed the voice of God.

It is written, "Now the Lord had said unto Abram, Get thee out of thy country, and from thy kindred, and from thy father's house, unto a land that I will shew thee: And I will make of thee a great nation, and I will bless thee, and make thy name great; and thou shalt be a blessing: And I will bless them that bless thee, and curse him that curseth thee: and in thee shall all families of the earth be blessed. So Abram departed, as the Lord had spoken unto him;….." **Genesis 12:1-4**

Unless *we develop the spirit of faithfulness,* we will forever miss the blessing of God upon our lives. Often we desire the blessing but lack the patience to wait for it. We are told in Galatians 6:9, "And let us not be weary in well doing: for in due season we shall reap, if we faint not.

Unless we obey God's divine instruction concerning our life in faith, we are not entitled to break-through in life. Unless we become faithful concerning God's promises concerning our life, we are not entitled to the blessing.

For the most part, our life will be full of struggle and toiling, until we locate God's plan, and purpose concerning our life. In my own opinion, we will suffer great calamity and destruction in life, if we do not follow God's pattern concerning our lives. In my own understanding, it takes *faithfulness to obey God*. I encourage you to continue and remain faithful to whatever He said for you to do in life. God is searching for men who are faithful, *"His lord said unto him, Well done, good and faithful servant; thou hast been faithful over a few things, I will make thee ruler over many things: enter thou into the joy of thy lord."* **Matthew 25:23**

It is our faithfulness in life that determines the impact we make in life. "Cast not away therefore your confidence, which hath great recompense of reward. For ye have need of patience, that, after ye have done the will of God, ye might receive the promise." **Hebrew 10:35-36**

Faithfulness is a character we covet in life. We want our spouse to be faithful to us in good times and bad times. It is written, "And if ye have not been faithful in that which is another man's, who shall give you that which is your own?" **(Luke 16:12)** As simple as faithfulness may sound, it is not easy to be faithful in times of economic recession. The bible told a graphic story of two women who agreed to eat their son for dinner one after another.

Although she ate the other woman's son for dinner, once it was her son's turn, she was un-faithful to bring her son for dinner. *"And the king said unto her, What aileth thee? And she answered, This woman said unto me, Give thy son, that we may eat him to day, and we will eat my son to morrow. So we boiled my son, and did eat him: and I said unto her on the next day, Give thy son, that we may eat him: and she hath hid her son."* **2 King 6:28-29**

Faithful men/women of God are *God fearing people*. Faithful men and women of God are men of impact that rule their world. Although it's not easy to be faithful people in this end time. *"He that is faithful in that which is least is faithful also in much: and he that is unjust in the least is unjust also in much. If therefore ye have not been faithful in the unrighteous mammon, who will commit to your trust the true riches? And if ye have not been faithful in that which is another man's, who shall give you that which is your own?"* **Luke 16:10-12**

What does it mean to remain faithful?

We are told....

"He that is faithful in that which is least is faithful also in much: and he that is unjust in the least is unjust also in much." **Luke 16:10**

To remain faithful, in my own simple interpretation, means to do what is right at all times, this includes to remain diligent, and hardworking to whatever assignment God gave you to do. It is written, *"Whatsoever thy hand findeth to do, do it with thy might; for there is no work, nor device, nor knowledge, nor wisdom, in the grave, whither thou goest."* **Eccl 9:10**

We must develop the attitude of gratefulness, joy, excitement, and hardworking at any little small thing He told us to do in life.

Remember....

"For who hath despised the day of small things?" **Zech 4:10**

"Though thy beginning was small, yet thy latter end should greatly increase." **Job 8:7**

Often very few church folks believe in hard work. As Christians our dignity is in hard work and our integrity. We must take responsibility for the outcome of our life. Jesus Himself was faithful and obedience to death. *"And being found in fashion as a man, he humbled himself, and became obedient unto death, even the death of the cross. Wherefore God also hath highly exalted him, and given him a name which is above every name:"* **Phi 2:8-9**

Unless you remain faithful and humbled in life, God will not exalt you. Jesus Christ Himself said I must work. If *Jesus the son of God was* determined to work, what are you doing with idleness? *"I must work the works of him that sent me, while it is day: the night cometh, when no man can work."* **John 9:4**

REQUIRED CONDITIONS TO OBEY DIVINE INSTRUCTION

~Repentance

Unless you repent, God will not restore. This is the first step into any kind of deliverance. If you cannot repent then you cannot be freed. *"From that time Jesus began to preach, and to say, Repent: for the kingdom of heaven is at hand."* (Matthew4:17). Unless you repent your obedience is fake. It is written, *"And saying, Repent ye: for the kingdom of heaven is at hand."* **Matthew 3:2**

~Be Baptized

Are you truly in the faith, then get baptized? Unless you are engrafted in the faith, you will forever remain a stranger to these mysteries. God want to use you to do great things, perhaps I'm talking to myself, but you must be baptized. "…. be baptized every one of you in the name of Jesus Christ for the remission of sins, and ye shall receive the gift of the Holy Ghost." Acts 2:38

~Confess of Your Sin

"Unless you let go of your sins by confession, you cannot let God into your heart." No one can fake obeying divine instructions. Whenever you obey God, it shows. Therefore, unless you confess your sins, you will forever remain a prayer topic. I urge you today to confess your sins, and make Jesus Christ, the Lord over your life. "Confession of our sins is the access key into possession." *"If we confess our sins, he is faithful and just to forgive us our sins, and to cleanse us from all unrighteousness."* **1 John 1:9**

~Acknowledgment

DO YOU KNOW HIM?

Often most people make me laugh, they claim to know of God, but they do not know His ways. We are told, *"And why call ye me, Lord, Lord, and do not the things which I say?"* Luke 6:46

Unless you obey God by acknowledging Him in all your endeavors, you will remain in charge of your life. But every time you acknowledge him, He take charge of your life. It is written, *"Because they regard not the works of the Lord, nor the operation of his hands, he shall destroy them, and not build them up."* Psalms 28:5

We were told....

"For I acknowledge my transgressions: and my sin is ever before me." Psalms 51:3

Furthermore....

"Behold, I was shapen in iniquity; and in sin did my mother conceive me." (Psalms 51:5) The truth of this mystery is that we must come into compliance in faith, in righteousness, if we must obey God. It is written, *"For all have sinned, and come short of the glory of God;"* (Romans 3:23)

Jesus is looking for men and women with a heart for God. Men and women willing to evangelize the good news of the gospel. Men and women with a heart of love for self and others. Unless your heart is right, your obedience is fake. "A son honoureth his father, and a servant his master: if then I be a father, where is mine honour? and if I be a master, where is my fear? saith the Lord of hosts unto you, O priests, that despise my name. And ye say, Wherein have we despised thy name?" (Mal 1:6) We must acknowledge the Lord in our lives.

BORN AGAIN

This is the mystery of the new birth experience that every believer must experience as we encounter Jesus as savior. Jesus made it clear to us all, we must be born again. Otherwise we are not in the faith. It is written, *"But as many as received him, to them gave he power to become the sons of God, even to them that believe on his name:"* **John 1:12** "Jesus answered and said unto him, Verily, verily, I say unto thee, Except a man be born again, he cannot see the kingdom of God." (John 3:3)

CONDITIONS FOR THE HELP OF THE HOLY SPIRIT

WALKING IN THE SPIRIT:

This simply means *to walk in obedience. For unless you obey you are heading into shame and destruction. Jesus took the shame and nailed it on the cross. Therefore look up to Jesus in faith and in obedience and he will direct your path in life.* "This I say then, Walk in the Spirit, and ye shall not fulfil the lust of the flesh." Gal 5:17

FAITH

However you may interpret it, any kind of obedience in life demands faith in God. It takes faith to obey the voice of God. Think of Abraham. Abraham obedience was a product of faith in God.

It is written....

"Now the Lord had said unto Abram, Get thee out of thy country, and from thy kindred, and from thy father's house, unto a land that I will shew thee: And I will make of thee a great nation, and I will bless thee, and make thy name great; and thou shalt be a blessing: And I will bless them that bless thee, and curse him that curseth thee: and in thee shall all families of the earth be blessed. So Abram departed, as the Lord had spoken unto him....." **Genesis 12:1-4** It takes faith to move into the miraculous. It takes faith in God to operate in signs and wonders in life.

"We having the same spirit of faith, according as it is written, I believed, and therefore have I spoken; we also believe, and therefore speak." 2 Cor 4:13

WALK IN AGREEMENT

ARE YOU WALKING IN AGREEMENT WITH GOD?

God has been trying to get your attention for a very long time. May I say this to you here? I know you love God but its time for you to agree and walk with God. *"Can two walk together, except they both agreed?"* (Amos 3:3) Unless you are in agreement with God, your walk and believe system is fake. *We must come in agreement with the voice of the Lord. We must walk in agreement with* the instructions of the Holy Spirit.

WALK IN LOVE

In my own opinion, *anyone walking in love is walking in obedience.* For it takes obedience to walk in love. " And we have known and believed the love that God hath to us. God is love; and he that dwelleth in love dwelleth in God, and God in him." (1 John 4:16) Literally anyone *can hear from the Spirit,* but unless you are in love, He will not reveal His secrets. Unless you are in love you will be confused which spirit is speaking to you. It is written, *"The secret of the Lord is with them that fear him; and he will shew them his covenant."* **Psalms 25:14**

WALK IN TRUTH

DO YOU GENUINELY WANT TO HEAR FROM GOD?

If your answer is "yes" then you must come in compliance with the truth of the word of God. It is only the truth that can set us free in life. "If the Son therefore shall make you free, ye shall be free indeed." (John 8:32) The truth is you must begin to obey divine instruction given to you in your dreams, revelation, through the word of God and through your God given prophets in life.

PREVAILING PRAYER POINTS

I cancel my name and that of my family from the death register, with the fire of God, in the name of Jesus.

Every weapon of destruction fashioned against me and my family, be destroyed by the fire of God, in the name of Jesus.

Power of God, fight for me in every area of my life, in Jesus' name.

Every hindrance to my breakthrough, be melted by the fire of God, in the name of Jesus.

Every evil power against me, be scattered by the thunder fire of God, in the name of Jesus.

Father Lord, destroy every evil man/woman in the name of Jesus.

Every failures of the past, be converted to success , in Jesus' name.

Father Lord, let the former rain, the latter rain and Your blessing pour down on me now.

Father Lord, let all the failure turn into success for me, in the name of Jesus.

I receive power from on high and I paralyze all the powers of darkness that are diverting my blessings, in the name of Jesus.

Beginning from this day, I employ the services of the angels of God to open unto me every door of opportunity and breakthroughs, in the name of Jesus.

I will not go around in circles again, I will make progress, in the name of Jesus.

I shall not build for another to inhabit and I shall not plant for another to eat, in the name of Jesus.

I paralyse the powers of the emptier concerning my handiwork, in the name of Jesus.

O Lord, let every locust, caterpillar and palmerworm assigned to eat the fruit of my labour be roasted by the fire of God.

The enemy shall not spoil my testimony in this programme, in the name of Jesus.

By the blood of Jesus, I reject every backward journey, in the name of Jesus.

By the blood of Jesus, I paralyze every strongman attached to any area of my life, in the name of Jesus.

I pray, Let every agent of shame fashioned to work against my life be paralyzed, in the name of Jesus.

I paralyse the activities of household wickedness over my life, in the name of Jesus.

I quench every strange fire emanating from evil tongues against me, in the name of Jesus.

Father Lord, give me power for maximum achievement.

Heavenly father, give me comforting authority to achieve my goal.

Blood of Jesus Christ, defend and fortify me with Your power.

I paralyse every spirit of disobedience in my life, in Jesus' name.

I refuse to disobey the voice of God, in the name of Jesus.

Every root of rebellion in my life, be uprooted, in Jesus' name.

By the blood of Jesus, I destroy every witchcraft spirit in my life, in the name of Jesus.

Contradicting forces promoting hindrance in my life, die, in Jesus' name.

Every inspiration of witchcraft in my family, be destroyed, in the name of Jesus.

Blood of Jesus, blot out every evil mark of witchcraft in my life, in the name of Jesus.

Every garment put upon me by witchcraft, be torn to pieces, in the name of Jesus.

Angels of God, begin to pursue my household enemies, let their ways be dark and slippery, in the name of Jesus.

Lord, confuse them and turn them against themselves.

By the blood of Jesus, I break every evil unconscious agreement with household enemies concerning my miracles, in the name of Jesus.

Household witchcraft, fall down and die, in the name of Jesus.

Father Lord, drag all the household wickedness to the Dead Sea and bury them there.

Father Lord, I reject to follow the evil pattern of remote control my household enemies.

My life, jump out from the cage of household wickedness, in the name of Jesus.

I command all my blessings and potentials buried by wicked household enemies to be exhumed, in the name of Jesus.

I will see the goodness of the Lord in the land of the living, in the name of Jesus.

Everything done against me to spoil my joy, receive destruction, in the name of Jesus.

Father Lord, as Abraham received favor in Your eyes, let me receive Your favor, so that I can excel in every area of my life.

Lord Jesus, help my shortcoming and infirmities in the name of Jesus.

It does not matter, whether I deserve it or not, I receive immeasurable favor from the Lord, in the name of Jesus.

By the blood of Jesus I receive every blessing God has apportioned to me in the name of Jesus.

My blessing will not be transferred to my neighbor in the name of Jesus.

Father Lord, disgrace every power that is tormenting my breakthrough in the name of Jesus.

Every step I take shall lead to outstanding success, in Jesus' name.

I shall prevail with man and with God in every area of my life, in the name of Jesus.

Every habitation of infirmity in my life, break to pieces, in the name of Jesus.

My body, soul and spirit, reject every evil load, in Jesus' name.

Evil foundation in my life, I pull you down today, in the mighty name of Jesus.

Every inherited sickness in my life, depart from me now, in the name of Jesus.

Every evil water in my body, get out, in the name of Jesus.

By the blood of Jesus, I cancel the effect of every evil dedication in my life, in the name of Jesus.

Holy Ghost fire, immunize my blood against satanic poisoning, in the name of Jesus.

Father Lord, put self control in my mouth, in the name of Jesus.

I refuse to get accustomed to sickness, in the name of Jesus.

Every door open to infirmity in my life, be permanently closed today, in the name of Jesus.

Every power contenting with God in my life, be roasted, in the name of Jesus.

Every power preventing God's glory from manifesting in my life, be paralysed, in the name of Jesus.

I loose myself from the spirit of desolation, in the name of Jesus.

Father Lord break me through in my home, in the name of Jesus.

Father Lord keep in me healthy, in the name of Jesus.

Father Lord break me through in my business, in the name of Jesus.

Let God be God in my economy, in the name of Jesus.

Glory of God, envelope every department of my life, in the name of Jesus.

The Lord that answereth by fire, be my God, in the name of Jesus.

By the blood of Jesus, all my enemies shall scatter to rise no more, in the name of Jesus.

Blood of Jesus, cry against all evil gatherings arranged for my sake, in the name of Jesus.

Father Lord, convert all my past failures to unlimited victories, in the name of Jesus.

Lord Jesus, create room for my advancement in every area of my life.

All evil thoughts against me, Lord turn them to be good for me.

Father Lord, destroy anyone that is against my life in the name of Jesus.

Father Lord, advertise Your dumbfounding prosperity in my life.

Let the showers of dumbfounding prosperity fall in every department of my life, in the name of Jesus.

By the blood of Jesus, I claim all my prosperity in the name of Jesus.

Every door of my prosperity that has been shut, be opened now, in the name of Jesus.

Father Lord, convert my poverty to prosperity, in the name of Jesus.

Father Lord, convert my mistake to perfection, in the name of Jesus.

Father Lord, convert my frustration to fulfillment, in the name of Jesus.

Father Lord, bring honey out of the rock for me, in the name of Jesus.

By the blood of Jesus, I stand against every evil covenant of sudden death, in the name of Jesus.

By the blood of Jesus, I break every conscious and unconscious evil covenant of untimely death, in the name of Jesus.

You spirit of death and hell, you have no document in my life, in the name of Jesus.

You stones of death, depart from my ways, in the name of Jesus.

Father Lord, make me a voice of deliverance and blessing.

By the blood of Jesus, I tread upon the high places of the enemies, in the name of Jesus.

I bind and render useless, every blood sucking demon, in the name of Jesus.

You evil current of death, loose your grip over my life, in the name of Jesus.

By the blood of Jesus, I frustrate the decisions of the evil openers in my family, in the name of Jesus.

Fire of protection, cover my family, in the name of Jesus.

Father Lord, make my way perfect, in the name of Jesus.

Throughout the days of my life, I shall not be put to shame, in the name of Jesus.

By the blood of Jesus, I reject every garment of shame, in the name of Jesus.

By the blood of Jesus, I reject every shoe of shame, in the name of Jesus.

By the blood of Jesus, I reject every head-gear and cap of shame, in the name of Jesus.

Shamefulness shall not be my lot, in the name of Jesus.

Every demonic limitation of my progress as a result of shame, be removed, in the name of Jesus.

Every network of shame around me, be paralysed, in the name of Jesus.

Those who seek for my shame shall die for my sake, in the name of Jesus.

As far as shame is concerned, I shall not record any point for satan, in the name of Jesus.

In the name of Jesus, I shall not eat the bread of sorrow, I shall not eat the bread of shame and I shall not eat the bread of defeat.

No evil will touch me throughout my life, in the name of Jesus.

By the blood of Jesus, In every area of my life, my enemies will not catch me, in the name of Jesus.

By the blood of Jesus, In every area of my life, I shall run and not grow weary, I shall walk and shall not faint.

Father Lord, in every area of my life, let not my life disgrace You.

By the blood of Jesus, I will not be a victim of failure and I shall not bite my finger for any reason, in the name of Jesus.

Holy Spirit of God, Help me O Lord, to meet up with God's standard for my life.

By the blood of Jesus, I refuse to be a candidate to the spirit of amputation, in the name of Jesus.

By the blood of Jesus, with each day of my life, I shall move to higher ground, in the name of Jesus.

Every spirit of shame set in motion against my life, I bind you, in the name of Jesus.

Every spirit competing with my breakthroughs, be chained, in the name of Jesus.

By the blood of Jesus, I bind every spirit of slavery, in the name of Jesus.

By the blood of Jesus, In every day of my life, I disgrace all my stubborn pursuers, in the name of Jesus.

By the blood of Jesus, I bind, every spirit of Herod, in the name of Jesus.

Every spirit challenging my God, be disgraced, in Jesus' name.

Every Red Sea before me, be parted, in the name of Jesus.

By the blood of Jesus, I command every spirit of bad ending to be bound in every area of my life, in the name of Jesus.

By the blood of Jesus, Every spirit of Saul, be disgraced in my life, in the name of Jesus.

By the blood of Jesus, Every spirit of Pharaoh, be disgraced in my life, in Jesus' name.

By the blood of Jesus, I reject every evil invitation to backwardness, in Jesus' name.

By the blood of Jesus, I command every stone of hindrance in my life to be rolled away, in the name of Jesus.

Father Lord, roll away every stone of poverty from my life, in the name Jesus.

Let every stone of infertility in my marriage be rolled away, in the name of Jesus.

Let every stone of non-achievement in my life be rolled away, in the name of Jesus.

My God, roll away every stone of hardship and slavery from my life, in the name of Jesus.

My God, roll away every stone of failure planted in my life, my home and in my business, in the name of Jesus.

You stones of hindrance, planted at the edge of my breakthroughs, be rolled away, in the name of Jesus.

You stones of stagnancy, stationed at the border of my life, be rolled away, in the name of Jesus.

Father Lord, I thank You for all the stones You have rolled away, I forbid their return, in the name of Jesus.

Let the power from above come upon me, in the name of Jesus.

Father Lord, advertise Your power in every area of my life, in the name of Jesus.

Father Lord, make me a power generator, throughout the days of my life, in the name of Jesus.

Let the power to live a holy life throughout the days of my life fall upon me, in the name of Jesus.

Let the power to live a victorious life throughout the days of my life fall upon me, in the name of Jesus.

Let the power to prosper throughout the days of my life fall upon me, in the name of Jesus.

Let the power to be in good health throughout the days of my life fall upon me, in the name of Jesus.

Let the power to disgrace my enemies throughout the days of my life fall upon me, in the name of Jesus.

Let the power of Christ rest upon me now, in the name of Jesus.

Let the power to bind and loose fall upon me now, in the name of Jesus.

Father Lord, let Your key of revival unlock every department of my life for Your revival fire, in the name of Jesus.

Every area of my life that is at the point of death, receive the touch of revival, in the name of Jesus.

Father Lord, send down Your fire and anointing into my life, in the name of Jesus.

Every uncrucified area in my life, receive the touch of fire and be crucified, in the name of Jesus.

Let the fire fall and consume all hindrances to my advancement, in the name of Jesus.

You stubborn problems in my life, receive the Holy Ghost dynamite, in the name of Jesus.

You carry-over miracle from my past, receive the touch of fire in the name of Jesus.

Holy Ghost fire, baptize me with prayer miracle, in Jesus' name.

By the blood of Jesus, Every area of my life that needs deliverance, receive the touch of fire and be delivered, in the name of Jesus.

Let my angels of blessing locate me now, in the name of Jesus.

Every satanic programme of impossibility, I cancel you now, in the name of Jesus.

Every household wickedness and its programme of impossibility, be paralysed, in the name of Jesus.

No curse will land on my head, in the name of Jesus.

Throughout the days of my life, I will not waste money on my health: the Lord shall be my healer, in the name of Jesus.

Throughout the days of my life, I will be in the right place at the right time.

Throughout the days of my life, I will not depart from the fire of God's protection, in the name of Jesus.

Throughout the days of my life, I will not be a candidate for incurable disease, in the name of Jesus.

Every weapon of captivity, be disgraced, in the name of Jesus.

Let every attack planned against the progress of my life be frustrated, in the name of Jesus.

I command the spirits of harassment and torment to leave me, in the name of Jesus.

Lord, begin to speak soundness into my mind and being.

I reverse every witchcraft curse issued against my progress, in the name of Jesus.

I condemn all the spirits condemning me, in the name of Jesus.

Let divine accuracy come into my life and operations, in the name of Jesus.

No evil directive will manifest in my life, in the name of Jesus.

Let the plans and purposes of heaven be fulfilled in my life, in the name of Jesus.

O Lord, bring to me friends that reverence Your name and keep all others away.

Let divine strength come into my life, in the name of Jesus.

Let every stronghold working against my peace be destroyed, in the name of Jesus.

Let the power to destroy every decree of darkness operating in my life fall upon me now, in the name of Jesus.

Lord, deliver my tongue from evil silence.

Lord, let my tongue tell others of Your life.

Lord, loose my tongue and use it for Your glory.

Lord, let my tongue bring straying sheep back to the fold.

Lord, let my tongue strengthen those who are discouraged.

Lord, let my tongue guide the sad and the lonely.

Lord, baptise my tongue with love and fire.

Let every unrepentant and stubborn pursuers be disgraced in my life, in the name of Jesus.

Let every iron-like curse working against my life be broken by the blood of Jesus, in the name of Jesus.

Let every problem designed to disgrace me receive open shame, in the name of Jesus.

Let every problem anchor in my life be uprooted, in Jesus' name.

Multiple evil covenants, be broken by the blood of Jesus, in the name of Jesus.

Multiple curses, be broken by the blood of Jesus, in Jesus' name.

Everything done against me with evil padlocks, be nullified by the blood of Jesus, in the name of Jesus.

Everything done against me at any cross-roads, be nullified by the blood of Jesus, in the name of Jesus.

Let every stubborn and prayer resisting demon receive stones of fire and thunder, in the name of Jesus.

Every stubborn and prayer resisting sickness, loose your evil hold upon my life, in the name of Jesus.

Every problem associated with the dead, be smashed by the blood of Jesus, in the name of Jesus.

I recover my stolen property seven fold, in the name of Jesus.

Let every evil memory about me be erased by the blood of Jesus, in the name of Jesus.

By the blood of Jesus, I disallow my breakthroughs from being caged, in Jesus' name.

Let the sun of my prosperity arise and scatter every cloud of poverty, in the name of Jesus.

I decree unstoppable advancement upon my life, in Jesus' name.

I soak every day of my life in the blood of Jesus and in signs and wonders, in the name of Jesus.

I break every stronghold of oppression in my life, in Jesus' name.

Let every satanic joy about my life be terminated, in the name of Jesus.

I paralyze every household wickedness, in the name of Jesus.

Let every satanic spreading river dry up by the blood of Jesus, in the name of Jesus.

I bind every ancestral spirit and command them to loose their hold over my life, in the name of Jesus.

WISDOM KEYS

— Every Productive Society is a society heading to the top.

— Millions of Nigerians run away from Nigeria, very few Nigerians stay in Nigeria.

— My decision to return Nigeria is the will of God for my life.

— My short coming in America after 18 years, trained me to be wise, to think, reflect and reason appropriately.

— If you train your mind to reason it will train your hands to earn money.

— It is absurd to use the money of the heathen to build the kingdom of the living God.

— Every Ministry reveals its agenda and goal either at the beginning or at the end. Be careful of your life it is your first Ministry.

— The average American mind is conditioned for a continual quest to get new things and (discard the former) and throw away old things.

— When I considered well, my BMW jeep became my initial deposit for the work of the ministry in Nigeria.

— Money will never fall from any tree.

— Everyone is waiting for you to change your mind until you change your thinking nothing changes around you.

— Multiple academic degrees in other discipline gave me the chance to think, reflect and reason.

— What so everyone are thinking and reflecting at the moment reveals you to the time and the now factor .

— All events and intents are the product of precise thought processes, accurate reason every event is designed for a designated timeline.

— Wisdom is your ability to think, to create and invent. If you can think wise enough you will come out of penury.

— The distance between you and success is your creative ability to think reason and reflect accurate.

— Success is the result of hard work, commitment resolve and determination learning from past mistakes and failing.

— If you organize your mind you have organized your life and destiny.

— There is a thin line between success and failure. If you look above and beyond you are on your way to success.

— Wealth is your ability to think, power is your ability to reason and success is your ability to be informed.

— If you can make use of your mind by thinking and reasoning God will make use of your life and destiny.

— Think and Be Great.

— Reflect, Reason, Think and Be Great.

— Famous people are born of woman.

— That you will make it is your intention; that you will survive is your resolve, that you will succeed with changes is your determination, personal efforts and hard work.

— No man was born a failure. Lack of vision is the end product of failure.

— Working with mental patients encourages and aspire me to be a productive observant and dedicated to my assignment.

— Successful people are not magicians, it is the will power combined with hard work, and determination and a resolve to succeed that make them succeed.

— In the unequivocal state of the mind, intention is not a location or a position it is the state of the mind.

— So many people think, that they think. The mind is used to think, reflect, and reason. You will remain blind with your eye open until you can see with your mind by thinking.

— There is no favoritism in accurate and precise calculation.

— Although knowledge is power, information is the key and gateway to a great future.

— It will take the hand of God to move the hand of man.

— With the backing of the great wise God, nothing will disconnect you from your inheritance.

— As long as you have wisdom and understanding of God, Satan and evil cannot manipulate your life and destiny.

— You have come this far by yourself judgment and decision you have made in the past, now lean and listen to God for another dimension of greatness.

— Great people are common people it is extra ordinary effort and the price of sacrifice that produces greatness.

— As a mental direct care worker I saw a great pastor and a motivational speaker within myself.

— Menial job does not reduce your self-worth, until you resolve to achieve greatness see greatness in all you do; you will never count in your community.

— The principle of Jesus will solve your gambling and addiction problems.

— The man of Jesus will lead you into heaven,

— Everyone have their self-appraisal and what they think about you. Until you discover yourself other opinion about you will alter the real you.

— Supervisors and directors are just a position in the chain of command in a work place. Never allow your supervisor hierarchy to alter your opinion about yourself.

— Everyone can come out of debt if they make up their mind.

— That I am not a decision maker at work does not diminish my contribution to my world.

— Although it appears like it was a poor decision to accept a direct care employment at a psychiatric hospital as I reflect of my nine years of experience, it became apparent that I have learnt and experienced enough for my next assignment in life.

— Self-encouragement and determination is a resolve of the heart.

— If you are determined to make a difference, and do the things that make a difference you will eventually make a difference.

— Good things do not come easy.

— Short cuts will cut your life short.

— Those who look ahead move ahead.

— Life is all about making an impact. In your life time strive to make an impact in your community.

— Make friends and connect with people who are moving ahead of you in life.

— If you can look around well you have come a long way in your life, made a lot of difference and realized a lot of success in life.

— If you are my old friend, hurry up to reach out to me before I become a stranger to you.

— Everything I am blessed with inspirations from God, that change my definition and interpretation of the world around me.

— I thought I was stagnant and lonely until I looked around and noticed my children running around and my wife cooking.

— At 40 I resigned my Job to seek the Lord forever.

— My ministry took a drastic rise to the top when the wisdom of God visited me with knowledge and understanding.

— You will be a better person, if you understand the characteristics of your personality – your mood swings, attitudes, and habits.

— It is the seed of love you sow into the heart of a child and a woman that you reap in due time.

— Love is not selfish, love share everything including the concealed secrets of the mind.

— As long as you have a prayer life and a bible; you will never feel lonely, rejected, and idle in the race of life.

— When good friends disconnect from you, let them go, they might have seen something new in a different direction.

— Confidence in yourself and in God is the only way to bring you out of captivity.

— Never train a child to waste his/her time.

— The mind is the greatest assets of a great future.

— You walk by common sense run by principles and fly by instruction.

— Those who fly in flight of life fly alone.

— Up in the air you are alone. No one can toll you accept the compass of knowledge and information.

— I have seen a towing vehicle I have seen a towing ship I have never seen a tolling airplane.

— I exercise my judgment and make a decision every minute of the day.

— Decisions are crucial, critical and vital with reference to your future.

— So many people wish for a great future. You can only work towards a great future.

— Your celebrity status began when you discovered your talent. What are you good at? Work at it with all commitment.

— Prayers will sustain you but the wisdom of God will prosper you.

— When I met Oyedepo, his teachings changed my perspective. But when I met Ibiyeomie; His teaching changed my perception.

— I will be successful in ministry if only I concentrate and focus my energy in the work of the ministry.

— It took the late Dr. Vincent Pearle Norman's book to open my mind towards kingdom success.

CHAPTER 3

PRAYER OF SALVATION

"Neither is there salvation in any other: for there is none other name under heaven given among men, whereby we must be saved."
Acts 4:12

The purpose of this book is to spread the word of God in print. The purpose is defeated if you do not accept the Lord as your personal savior and Lord over your life. Unless you are saved, your hearing channels are not secured. Every time you are not saved, just about any contrary spirit can mislead you. If God must lead you, then you must obey the voice of God and be saved.

What must I do to determine my divine visitation?

To determine divine visitation you must be born again! The word says as many as received him, to them gave He power to become the sons of God. Even to them that believe on his name.

To qualify for divine visitation, do the following with sincerity—

1) Acknowledge that you are a sinner and that He died for you. (Romans 3:23)

2) Repent of your sins. (Acts 3:19, Luke 13:5, 2 Peter 3:9)

3) Believe in your heart that Jesus died for your sin. (Romans 10:10)

4) Confess Jesus as the Lord over your life. (Romans 10:10, Acts 2:21)

"Therefore if any man be in Christ, he is a new creature: old things are passed away; behold, all things are become new." 2 Cor 5:17

Now repeat this Prayer after me

Say Lord Jesus, I accept you today, as my Lord and my savior, forgive me of my sins wash me with your blood. Right now, I believe, I am sanctified, I am save, I am free, I am free from the Power of sin to serve the Lord Jesus. Thank you Lord for saving me. Amen.

Congratulations: You are now...

A BORN AGAIN CHRISTIAN.

Again I say to you—

CONGRATULATIONS!

I adjure you to watch the Spirit of God bear witness with your Spirit confirming His word with signs following. The word says The Spirit itself beareth witness with our spirit, that we are the children of God.

MIRACLE CARE OUTREACH

"...But that the members should have the same care one for another"
1 Corinthians 12:25

We are all members of the body of Christ. Jesus commanded us to love our neighbor as ourselves. This includes caring for one another as a member of one body. True love is expressed in caring and giving. The word says for God so Love He gave....

Reach out to someone in need of Jesus, help someone in crisis find Christ. Look out and prove your love to Jesus by caring and inviting your friends and associates to find Jesus the Healer.

Invite your friends to our Home Care Cell Fellowship (Miracle chapel Intl Satellite fellowship) In the USA at 33 Schley Street Newark New Jersey 07112. Home Care Cell fellowship Group meets every Tuesday at 6:00pm-7:00pm.

If you are in Nigeria—**MIRACLE OF GOD MINISTRIES**, aka **"MIRACLE CHAPEL INTL"** Mpama –Egbu-Owerri Imo state Nigeria.

LIFE IS NOT ALL ABOUT DURATION—
BUT ITS ALL ABOUT DONATION

What does the above statement mean?....

Life consists not in the accumulation of material wealth. (Luke 12:15) But it's all about liberality...meaning - what you can give and share with others. Proverb 11:25. When you live for others—You live forever - because you out live your generation by the legacy you live behind after you depart into glory to be with the Lord. But when you live to yourself - you are reduced to self—you are easily forgotten when you die and depart in glory. Permit me to admonish you today to live your life to be a blessing to a soul connected to you today. I want you to know that so many souls are connected and looking up to you, and through you so many souls will be saved and rescued from destruction. Will you disciple someone today to find Jesus Christ?

As a genuine Christian; it is your duty to evangelize Jesus Christ to all you meet on your way. Jesus is still in the healing business-Jesus is still doing miracles from time of old to now. Therefore tell someone about Jesus Christ today, disciple and bring them to Church. (John 1:45) Philip findeth Nathanael....

Please to prove the sincerity of your love for God today; please become a soul winner. The dignity of your Christianity is hidden in your boldness to proclaim and evangelize Jesus Christ to all you meet on your way. There is a question mark on the integrity of your Christianity until you become a life soul winner. Invite someone to join us worship the Lord Jesus this coming Sunday. Amen.

MIRACLE OF GOD MINISTRIES

PILLARS OF THE COMMISSION

We Believe Preach and Practice the following:

1) We believe and preach Salvation to every living human being

2) We believe and preach Repentance and forgiveness of sins

3) We believe and preach the baptism of the Holy Spirit and Spiritual gifts

4) We believe and teach the Prosperity

5) We believe and preach Divine Healing and Miracles (Signs & Wonder)

6) We believe and preach Faith

7) We believe and proclaim the Power of God (Supernatural)

8) We believe and proclaim Praise & Worship to God

9) We believe and preach Wisdom

10) We believe and preach Holiness (Consecration)

11) We believe and preach Vision

12) We believe and teach the Word of God

13) We believe and teach Success

14) We believe and practice Prayer

15) We believe and teach Deliverance

These 15 stones form the Pillars of Our Commission. Become part of this church family and follow this great move of God.

MY HEART FELT PRAYER FOR YOU

It is my desire that you develop a relationship and fellowship with the Holy Spirit of promise. It is also my desire that you encounter God through the pages of this book or any of my other spiritual literature. Or from any other established Christian author. May you experience God in a new way, in Jesus Mighty Name.

Heavenly Father, may today be a day of encounter with your spirit. Lord visit this precious one reading book and change their story in the Mighty Name of Jesus. Amen

What must I do to determine my divine visitation?

To determine divine visitation you must be born again! The word says as many as received him, to them gave He power to become the sons of God. Even to them that believe on his name.

To qualify for divine visitation, do the following with sincerity—

1) Acknowledge that you are a sinner and that He died for you. (Romans 3:23)

2) Repent of your sins. (Acts 3:19, Luke 13:5, 2 Peter 3:9)

3) Believe in your heart that Jesus died for your sin. (Romans 10:10)

4) Confess Jesus as the Lord over your life. (Romans 10:10, Acts 2:21)

"Therefore if any man be in Christ, he is a new creature: old things are passed away; behold, all things are become new." 2 Cor 5:17

Now repeat this Prayer after me

Say Lord Jesus, I accept you today, as my Lord and my savior, forgive me of my sins wash me with your blood. Right now, I believe, I am sanctified, I am save, I am free, I am free from the Power of sin to serve the Lord Jesus. Thank you Lord for saving me. Amen.

Congratulations: You are now...

A BORN AGAIN CHRISTIAN.

Again I say to you—

CONGRATULATIONS!

I guarantee you! Watch the Spirit of God bear witness with your Spirit confirming His word with signs following. The word says The Spirit itself beareth witness with our spirit, that we are the children of God. Join a bible believing church or join us on our weekly and Sunday worship services at 343 Sanford Avenue Newark New Jersey 07106.

CONCLUSION

"Out of heaven he made thee to hear his voice, that he might instruct thee: and upon earth he shewed thee his great fire; and thou heardest his words out of the midst of the fire." **Deut 4:36**

DO YOU GENUINELY WANT TO HEAR FROM GOD?

Although repentance is the key into deliverance, and promotion in life. If you must hear from the throne, then you must repent of your sins. Unless you change the way you think, you cannot change the outcome of your life. For every one that desired to encounter testimonies in life, we must change the way we think in our heart, confess the Lord Jesus, and forsake our sinful ways.

"Let us hear the conclusion of the whole matter: Fear God, and keep his commandments: for this is the whole duty of man. For God shall bring every work into judgment, with every secret thing, whether it be good, or whether it be evil." **Eccl1 2:13-14**

This book will remain a story to anyone who is not ready to make a decision for Jesus Christ. One man said if you failed to plan you have planned to fail in life. We want you to make plans to make heaven. The bible says "For God shall bring every work into judgment, with every secret thing, whether it be good, or whether it be evil." (Eccl1 2:14) If you are a born again Christian; we like to encourage you in your Christian life. If you are not a born again Christian we can help you here receive genuine salvation.

MEET HIM IN PRAYERS

Prayer is a two-way channel of communication. It is called a dialogue and not a monologue. Often some folks just want to air their heart and do not want to listen for what He will say to you. It is written, *"I will stand upon my watch, and set me upon the tower, and will watch to see what he will say unto me, and what I shall answer when I am reproved."* **Habakkuk 2:1** Every time we pray we must listen to what He will say to us

"And the Lord answered me, and said, Write the vision, and make it plain upon tables, that he may run that readeth it." **Habakkuk 2:2**

Unless we turn to God in prayers, we will miss our great future in life. God is the source of life. If we must *obey divine plan*, we must turn to God in prayers, and in thanksgiving in life. We must always be determined to pray until we breakthrough in life. We must repent of our sins, and take advantage of the greatest opportunity of salvation in life. It is written, *"If my people, which are called by my name, shall humble themselves, and pray, and seek my face, and turn from their wicked ways; then will I hear from heaven, and will forgive their sin, and will heal their land."* **2 Chronicle 7:14**

We are told *"Woe unto him that striveth with his Maker! Let the potsherd strive with the potsherds of the earth. Shall the clay say to him that fashioneth it, What makest thou? or thy work, He hath no hands?"* **(Isaiah 45:9)**

We must return to God with a genuine repented hearted, for our salvation and for the favor of God upon our lives. If there are any constant prevailing challenges against your life, *I pray in the Name of Jesus, let the power of God subdue the wicked one against your life even now in the Mighty Name of Jesus.* Amen. You can call 973-393-8518 for immediate prayer right now. Amen.

CHAPTER 4

ABOUT THE AUTHOR

Rev Franklin N Abazie is the founding and Presiding Pastor of Miracle of God Ministries with headquarters in Newark, New Jersey USA and a branch church in Owerri- Imo State Nigeria. He is following the footsteps of one of his mentors, Oral Roberts (Healing Evangelist) of the blessed memory. The Lord passed Oral Roberts healing mantle two days before he went to be with the Lord at age 91 into the hand of healing evangelist-Rev Franklin N Abazie in a vision.

In all his services the Power and Presence of God is present to heal all in his audience. He is an ordained man of God with a Healing Ministry reviving the healing and miracle ministry of Jesus Christ of Nazareth.

Pastor Franklin N Abazie, is called by God with a unique mandate: **"THE MOMENT IS DUE TO IMPACT YOUR WORLD THROUGH THE REVIVAL OF THE HEALING & MIRACLE MINISTRY OF JESUS CHRIST OF NAZARETH**

"I AM SENDING YOU TO RESTORE HEALTH UNTO THEE AND I

WILL HEAL THEE OF THY WOUNDS. SAID THE LORD OF HOST"

Rev. Abazie is a gifted ardent Teacher of the word of God who operates also in the office of a Prophet, generating and attracting undeniable signs & wonders, special miracles and healings, with apostolic fireworks of the Holy Ghost. He is the founding and presiding senior Pastor of this fast growing Healing ministry. He has written over 86 inspirational, healing and transforming books covering almost all aspect of divine healing and life. He is happily married and blessed with children.

BOOKS BY REV FRANKLIN N ABAZIE

1) The Outcome of Faith
2) Understanding the secret of prevailing Prayers
3) Commanding Abundance
4) Understanding the secret of the man God uses
5) Activating my due Season
6) Overcoming Divine Verdicts
7) The Outcome of Divine Wisdom
8) Understanding God's Restoration Mandate
9) Walking in the Victory and Authority of the truth
10) Gods Covenant Exemption
11) Destiny Restoration Pillars
12) Provoking Acceptable Praise
13) Understanding Divine Judgment
14) Activating Angelic Re-enforcement
15) Provoking Un-Merited Favor
16) The Benefits of the Speaking faith
17) Understanding Divine Arrangement
18) Put your faith to work
19) Developing a positive attitude in life
20) The Power of Prevailing faith
21) Inexplicable faith
22) The intellectual components of Redemption.
23) Dominating Controlling Spirit
24) Understanding Divine Prosperity
25) Understanding the secret of the man God Uses
26) Retaining Your Inheritance
27) Never give up hope
28) Commanding Angelic Escorts
29) The winner's faith
30) Understanding Your Guardian Angels
31) Overcoming the Dominion of Sin
32) Understanding the Voice of God

33) The Outstanding benefits of the Anointing
34) The Audacity of the Blood of Jesus
35) Walking in the Reality of the Anointing
36) The Mystery of Divine supply
37) Understanding Your Harvest Season
38) Activating Your Success Buttons
39) Overcoming the forces of Darkness
40) Overcoming the devices of the devil
41) Overcoming Demonic agents
42) Overcoming the sorrows of failure
43) Rejecting the Sorrows of failure
44) Resisting the Sorrows of Poverty
45) The Restoring broken Marriages.
46) Redeeming Your Days
47) The force of Vision
48) Overcoming the forces of ignorance
49) Understanding the sacrifice of small beginning
50) The might of small beginning
51) Praying in the Spirit
52) Dominating controlling Spirits
53) Breaking the shackles of the curse of the law
54) Covenant keys to answered prayers
55) Wisdom for Signs & Wonders
56) Wisdom for generational Impact
57) Wisdom for Marriage Stability
58) Understanding the number of your Days
59) Enforcing Your Kingdom Rights
60) Escaping the traps of immoralities
61) Escaping the trap of Poverty
62) Accessing Biblical Prosperity
63) Accessing True Riches in Christ
64) Silencing the Voice of the Accuser
65) Overcoming the forces of oppositions
66) Quenching the voice of the avenger
67) Silencing demonic Prediction & Projection

68) Silencing Your Mocker
69) Understanding the Power of the Holy Ghost
70) Understanding the baptism of Power
71) The Mystery of the Blood of Jesus
72) Understanding the Mystery of Sanctification
73) Understanding the Power of Holiness
74) Praying in the spirit
75) Activating the Forces of Vengeance
76) Appreciating the Mystery of Restoration
77) Covenant Keys to Answered Prayers
78) Engaging the mystery of the blood
79) Commanding the Power of the Speaking faith
80) Uprooting the forces against Your Rising
81) Overcoming mere success syndrome
82) Understanding Divine Sentence
83) Understanding the Mystery of Praise
84) Understanding the Author of Faith
85) The Mystery of the finisher of faith
86) Where is your trust?

MIRACLE OF GOD MINISTRIES

*NIGERIA CRUSADE
2012*

MIRACLE OF GOD MINISTRIES

NIGERIA CRUSADE 2012

MIRACLE OF GOD MINISTRIES

*NIGERIA CRUSADE
2012*

www.ingramcontent.com/pod-product-compliance
Lightning Source LLC
Chambersburg PA
CBHW021444080526
44588CB00009B/689